COGAT®
GRADE 5 TEST PREP

- Grade 5 Level 11 Form 7
- One Full Length Practice Test
- 176 Practice Questions
- Answer Key
- Sample Questions for Each Test Area
- 54 Additional Bonus Questions Online

Nicole Howard

PLEASE LEAVE US A REVIEW!

Thank you for selecting this book.

We'd love to get your feedback on the website where you purchased this book.

By leaving a review, you give us the opportunity to improve our work.

Nicole Howard and the SkilledChildren.com Team

www.skilledchildren.com

Co-authors: Albert Floyd and Steven Beck

TABLE OF CONTENTS

INTRODUCTION.. 5

Which Students Are Eligible to Take the CogAT Level 11?5

When in the School Year Does the CogAT Take Place? 6

An Overview of the CogAT Level 11 6

The Length and the Complete Format of the Test 7

The Test Breakdown 7

How to Use the Content in This Book 9

Tips and Strategies for Test Preparation 10

Before You Start Test Preparation.. 10

PRACTICE TEST VERBAL BATTERY 11

Verbal Analogies.. 12

Tips for Solving Verbal Analogies 12

Verbal Classification... 19

Tips for Solving Verbal Classification Questions................. 19

Sentence Completion 25

Tips for Sentence Completion.. 25

PRACTICE TEST NON VERBAL BATTERY 33

Figure Matrices... 34

Tips for Figure Matrices 34

Figure Classification... 43

Tips for Figure Classification 43

Paper Folding.. 55

Tips for Paper Folding 55

PRACTICE TEST QUANTITATIVE BATTERY 65

Number Puzzle 66

Tips for Number Puzzle... 66

Number Analogies... 72

Tips for Number Analogies 72

Number Series 78

Tips for Number Series 78

ANSWER KEY 85

Verbal Analogies Practice Test 86

Verbal Classification Practice Test 90

Sentence Completion Practice Test... 93

Figure Matrices Practice Test 96

Figure Classification Practice Test 99

Paper Folding Practice Test 102

Number Puzzle Practice Test 106

Number Analogies Practice Test 108

Number Series Practice Test 111

HOW TO DOWNLOAD 54 BONUS QUESTIONS 114

INTRODUCTION

The Cognitive Abilities Test (CogAT) is a K-12 evaluation of students' reasoning and problem-solving abilities through a battery of verbal, quantitative, and non-verbal test questions, published by Riverside Insights.

This book will provide an overview of the different types of questions related to grade 5, level 11, form 7 of the CogAT® test, and will increase a student's chances of success.

One complete practice test and the associated answer key, with clear clarifications, are all included in this book to help students better understand the structure of the test and the different question types within it.

Additionally, by reading this book, you gain free online access to 54 bonus practice questions. You will find the link and password on the last page of this book.

Please, read this introductory section to understand how the CogAT® works.

Which Students Are Eligible to Take the CogAT Level 11?

This book is dedicated to gifted eleven-year-old children and therefore focuses on level 11, form 7 of CogAT®. These tests will determine whether specific grade 5 students are ready to take the test.

CogAT® Level 11 is implemented by most Grade 5 teachers to identify which of their students will benefit from faster curriculum training modules. Used as a starting evaluation, it delivers reasonably accurate results.

When in the School Year Does the CogAT Take Place?

There is no fixed schedule for this specific type of test and CogAT® can be implemented when some districts or schools believe it is appropriate. Several school districts choose to implement these tests closer to the conclusion of the school year for more reliable and accurate results. If you are the parent or teacher of a student who could potentially qualify for this test, you will probably need to consult your school to determine how to sign a child for this test.

An Overview of the CogAT Level 11

The CogAT® is administered to a group of students at a single time.

There are three autonomous sections of the test, specifically:

1. Verbal testing

2. Nonverbal testing

3. Quantitative testing

These autonomous sections can be used individually, and some students may only be asked to take one or two parts of the test based on the evaluations of their tutors.

Although there are resources that support students prepare for these tests, the content of the CogAT® isn't generally the same content that is seen in the conventional school curriculum, and students will be asked to think creatively to solve certain questions.

The Length and the Complete Format of the Test

The total time given for the three sections of the Level 11 test is 90 minutes (30 minutes for each section).

Tests will vary, depending on the grades that are being assessed, but the Level 11 CogAT® is divided into 176 multiple-choice questions. The questions are categorized as follows:

Verbal Section

- "Sentence completion" has 20 questions.

- "Verbal classification" has 20 questions.

- "Verbal analogies" has 24 questions.

Nonverbal Section

- "Figure matrices" has 22 questions.

- "Paper folding skills" has 16 questions.

- "Figure classifications" has 22 questions.

Quantitative Section

- "Understanding number analogies" has 18 questions.

- "The number series" has 18 questions.

- "Solving number puzzles" has 16 questions.

The total number of questions for these three sections equals 176.

The Test Breakdown

The verbal section of the test is designed to assess a student's vocabulary, ability to solve problems associated with vocabulary, ability to determine word relationships, and their overall memory retention. The verbal section of the Level 11 CogAT® has three subtypes of questions that need to be answered:

1. Sentence Completion: Students are required to select words that accurately complete sentences in this section. This tests their knowledge of vocabulary.

2. Verbal Classification: Students are required to classify words into like groups in this section. They will be given three words that have something in common, and will be asked to identify a fourth word that completes the set. Each question in this section will have five possible answers for the students to choose from.

3. Verbal Analogies: Students are required to identify analogies. They will be given two words that go together (e.g. "dog" and "mammal") as well as a third, unrelated word. They must pick the most fitting pair for the third word from the answer choices given, based on the logic used for the original pair of words.

The nonverbal section of the test is designed to assess a student's ability to reason and think beyond what they've already been taught. This section includes geometric shapes and figures that aren't normally seen in the classroom. This will force the students to use different methods to try and solve problems. There are also three subtypes of questions that need to be answered in the nonverbal section of the CogAT:

1. Figure Classification: Students are required to analyze three similar figures and apply the next appropriate figure to complete the sequence in this section.

2. Figure Matrices: Students are introduced to basic matrices (2x2 grids) to solve for the missing shapes within them. Three of the four squares will already be filled out, and they must choose which image fills the last square from the options provided. This is similar to the verbal analogies section, except it is now done using shapes instead of words.

3. Paper Folding Skills: Students are introduced to paper folding and will need to ascertain where punched holes in a folded piece of paper would be after the paper is unfolded.

The quantitative section introduces abstract reasoning and problem-solving skills to learners and is one of the most challenging sections in the test. This section is also structured into three different parts:

1. Interpreting a Series of Numbers: Students are required to determine which number or numbers are needed to complete a series that follows a specific pattern.

2. Solving Number Puzzles: Students will need to solve number puzzles and simple equations. They will be provided with equations that are missing a number.

3. Understanding Number Analogies: Students are introduced to number analogies and will be required to determine what numbers are missing from the number sets. This is similar to figure matrices and verbal analogies.

How to Use the Content in This Book

Since the CogAT® is an important test in all students' schooling careers, the correct amount of preparation must be performed. Students that take the time to adequately prepare will inevitably do better than students that don't.

This book will help you prepare your student(s) before test day and will expose them to the format of the test so they'll know what to expect. This book includes:

- One full-length CogAT® Level 11 practice questionnaire.

- Question examples for teachers/parents to help their students approach all of the questions on the test with confidence and determination.

- Answer key with clear explanations.

Take the time to adequately go through all of the sections to fully understand how to teach this information to younger students. Many of the abstract versions of these questions will be difficult for some students to understand, so including some visual aids during preparation times will be greatly beneficial.

Tips and Strategies for Test Preparation

The most important factor regarding the CogAT® is to apply the time and effort to the learning process for the test and make the preparation periods as stress-free as possible. Although everyone will experience stress in today's world, being able to cope with that stress will be a useful tool throughout their lives. All students will experience varying amounts of anxiety and stress before these types of tests, but one of the ways to adequately combat this is by taking the time to prepare for them.

The CogAT® has difficult questions from the very beginning. Some of the questions will range from difficult to very abstract, regardless of the age group or level.

It's necessary to encourage your students to use different types of strategies to answer questions that they find challenging. Perfection should be aimed for, but isn't necessary on this test to still do very well. It's important for students to understand that to avoid overwhelming them.

Students will get questions incorrect in some of the sections, so it's vital to help younger students understand what errors they made so they can learn from their mistakes.

Before You Start Test Preparation

There are multiple factors that may stress students out, regardless of their age and maturity levels. It's imperative for you as an educator to help your students cope with the anxiety and stress of upcoming tests. The tests themselves are going to be stressful, but there are other, external factors that can increase the amounts of stress that children experience.

The first aspect that needs to be focused on is teaching the learners how to deal with stress. Breathing techniques are important, and having a quiet place to use when studying is imperative to decreasing the amount of stress that students experience.There are other aspects that can help alleviate stress, like teaching your students what pens and pencils they need to bring on the day and how to successfully erase filled out multiple-choice questions on the test questionnaire.

PRACTICE TEST VERBAL BATTERY

This section is designed to assess a student's vocabulary, ability to solve problems associated with vocabulary, ability to determine word relationship and memory retention.

Verbal Analogies

A verbal analogy traces a similarity between a pair of words and another pair of words.

Example

butterfly ⟶ insect : snake ⟶

A reptile   **B** insect   **C** bird   **D** fish   **E** amphibian

- First, identify the relationship between the first pair of words.
- How do the words "butterfly" and "insect" go together?

Scientists have classified the animals into classes to simplify their study.

Butterflies are Insects. "Insect" is a category.

- Now, look at the word "snake".
- Which of the possible choices follows the previous rule?

Snake is a reptile, so the correct answer is A.

Tips for Solving Verbal Analogies

- Try to identify the correlation between the first two words.
- Review all answers before you make a choice.
- Remove any word in the answers that don't have a comparable kind of relationship.
- Also, evaluate the possible alternative meanings of the words.

1.
actor → stage : skater →

A theater   **B** radio   **C** street   **D** lake
E rink

2.
cat → mouse: bird →

A snake   **B** flower   **C** worm   **D** egg   **E** milk

3.
migrain → brain : cataract →

A eye   **B** leg   **C** arm   **D** head   **E** hand

4.
botany → plants : zoology →

A flowers   **B** animals   **C** planets   **D** fruits
E fertilizers

5.

switch → light : key →

A airport **B** language **C** word **D** ignition
E helicopter

6.

head → neck : hand →

A nose **B** bone **C** knee **D** wrist **E** leg

7.

sweater → yarn : snowball →

A flower **B** snow **C** candy **D** rain **E** lower

8.

surgeon → scalpel : tailor →

A sword **B** knife **C** pen **D** metal **E** needle

9.
hand ⟶ grasp : arm ⟶

A think   **B** reach   **C** buy   **D** sing   **E** speak

10.
chemistry ⟶ chemist : zoology ⟶

A biology   **B** animals   **C** zoologist   **D** plants
E zoo

11.
tree ⟶ bark : bird ⟶

A feather   **B** silk   **C** wood   **D** water   **E** snow

12.
naive ⟶ experience : ⟶ illiterate

A success   **B** education   **C** elegance   **D** beauty
E wealth

13.

darkness ⟶ dark : heaviness ⟶

A weight   **B** heavy   **C** light   **D** sun   **E** lightness

14.

barber ⟶ hair : lumberjack ⟶

A sea   **B** flower   **C** ribbon   **D** tree   **E** rope

15.

God ⟶ eternal : mortal ⟶

A dissolute   **B** fleeting   **C** useless   **D** small
E voluminous

16.

young ⟶ robust : old ⟶

A good   **B** weak   **C** strong   **D** new   **E** high

17.

oasi → desert : island →

A field   **B** desert   **C** lake   **D** sky   **E** ocean

18.

hand→ human : feeler→

A insect   **B** snake   **C** giraffe   **D** dog   **E** octopus

19.

comedy → humorous : tragedy →

A romantic   **B** gloomy   **C** old   **D** ridiculous
E horrifying

20.

water→thirsty : food →

A liquid   **B** strong   **C** poisonous   **D** starving
E good

21.

scientist ⟶ laboratory : teacher ⟶

A gym   **B** labyrinth   **C** classroom   **D** math
E house

22.

drive ⟶ drove : eat ⟶

A food   **B** ate   **C** eating   **D** hungry   **E** eaten

23.

museum ⟶ painting : library ⟶

A room   **B** book   **C** notebook   **D** sheet   **E** page

24.

bald ⟶ hair : anemic ⟶

A sleep   **B** energy   **C** fur   **D** ageing   **E** weakness

Verbal Classification

Verbal classification questions ask the student to choose the voice that belongs to a group of three words.

Example

fennel, spinach, lettuce

A pear   **B** carrot   **C** apple   **D** banana   **E** cherry

- First, identify the relationship between the three words in the first row.
- What do the words fennel, spinach and lettuce have in common?

Fennel, spinach and lettuce are all vegetables.

- Now, look at the five worlds: pear, carrot, apple, banana, cherry. Which word goes best with the three words in the top row?

Carrot is also a vegetable, so the correct answer is B.

Tips for Solving Verbal Classification Questions

- Try to identify the correlation between the three words in the top row.
- Review all answers before you make a choice.
- Remove every word in the answers that don't have any kind of relationship with the three words in the top row.
- Also, evaluate the possible alternative meanings of the words.

1.
math, literature, history

A book   **B** science   **C** library   **D** house
E museum

2.
influenza, measles, chicken pox

A headache   **B** ebola   **C** stomachache
D sleepiness   **E** smartness

3.
jump, sell, explore,

A vision   **B** sunglasses   **C** run   **D** telescope
E microscope

4.
who, whose, which

A this   **B** what   **C** where   **D** whereas   **E** that

5.
sepal, petal, peduncle

A trunk   **B** pistil   **C** leg   **D** skin   **E** bark

6.
good, bad, nice

A strange   **B** goodness   **C** absurdity   **D** beauty
E fairness

7.
north, east, south

A under   **B** west   **C** below   **D** left   **E** right

8.
brain, liver, heart

A nose   **B** head   **C** ear   **D** stomach   **E** foot

9.

canoe, raft, barge

A duck   **B** ship   **C** car   **D** bicycle   **E** tractor

10.

residence, edifice, lodging

A position   **B** ship   **C** height   **D** width   **E** house

11.

coffee, water, wine

A tea   **B** silk   **C** oxygen   **D** concrete   **E** gas

12.

dove, finch, blackbird

A dog   **B** penguin   **C** tiger   **D** dolphin   **E** bear

13.
cat, gorilla, tiger

A sparrow   **B** snake   **C** dolphin   **D** turtle
E spider

14.
Arctic, Pacific, Indian

A Atlantic   **B** Gulf of Mexico   **C** Greenland
D Ireland   **E** Mediterranean Sea

15.
snake, chameleon, turtle

A snail   **B** frog   **C** lizard   **D** bat   **E** worm

16.
car, motorcycle, tractor

A bike   **B** cable car   **C** helicopter   **D** ship
E sled

17.
English, Spanish, Russian

A Belgium   **B** Italy   **C** Brazil   **D** China
E Italian

18.
heptagon, square, triangle

A pyramid   **B** hexagon   **C** cube   **D** sphere
E cone

19.
rake, spade, hoe

A sword   **B** knife   **C** wheelbarrow   **D** drill
E hammer

20.
wall, floor, ceiling

A door   **B** garden   **C** drainpipe   **D** guttering
E cellar

Sentence Completion

Complete the phrase using the appropriate word that best fits the meaning of the sentence as a whole.

Example

Dog owners must be _____ for controlling their animals.

A responsible   **B** new   **C** young   **D** amazing   **E** dangerous

- First, read the sentence. You will realize that one word is missing.
- Look at the answer choices under the main sentence. Which word would go better in the phrase?

Responsible= having an obligation to do something. Therefore, the right choice is "A".

Tips for Sentence Completion

- First, read the incomplete phrase.
- Think about what type of word you can use and try to anticipate the answer.
- Remove every word in the answers that don't have any kind of relationship with the main sentence.
- Read the incomplete sentence again.

1.

The Medical Research Council said it could not _____ the use of the new drug without further tests.

A sell   **B** attack   **C** approve   **D** win   **E** remove

2.

The country's natural resources have not yet been fully _____.

A exploited   **B** sold   **C** bought   **D** beloved
E eaten

3.

Journalists _____ on information from many different sources.

A calculate   **B** construct   **C** teach   **D** draw
E demolish

4.

The company has developed a new way to _____ solar energy.

A remove   **B** eat   **C** utilize   **D** connect   **E** steal

5.

In order to survive human beings need to _____ food and water.

A sell   **B** consume   **C** create   **D** love   **E** calculate

6.

The drug is _____ directly into the base of the spine.

A created   **B** brought   **C** injected   **D** removed
E hidden

7.

Jennifer was _____ that the magazine had agreed to publish one of her stories.

A depressed   **B** tired   **C** sad   **D** proud   **E** bored

8.
My parents used to say that their son would have the best education they could _____.

A save   **B** delete   **C** afford   **D** sell   **E** direct

9.
She's a good manager, because she _____ avoids dealing with the problems of her staff.

A always   **B** never   **C** continuously   **D** yesterday
E repeatedly

10.
Copernicus _____ in part the discoveries of the 17th and 18th centuries.

A refuse   **B** suspect   **C** rejected   **D** sell
E anticipated

11.

Two girls were _____ from school for taking drugs.

A killed   **B** held   **C** expelled   **D** kissed   **E** called

12.

You can imagine my _____ when I saw my sister's photograph on a magazine cover

A surprise   **B** sadness   **C** depression   **D** boredom
E anxiety

13.

Doctors had to use a metal rod to ___ the two pieces of bone together.

A detach   **B** load   **C** overlap   **D** join   **E** mix

14.

In all ages prior to our modern scientific age, people had a more physical and _____ lifestyle.

A new   **B** old   **C** funny   **D** active   **E** nice

15.
Volcanoes can remain _____ for hundreds of years.

A nice   **B** classical   **C** dirty   **D** big   **E** dormant

16.
A slight trembling of his hands _____ his growing excitement.

A mask   **B.** destroyed   **C** revealed   **D** pushed
E favored

17.
Several voluntary organizations are involved in providing community _____.

A tax   **B** discussions   **C** quarrels   **D** care
E fruits

18.
It's pretty _____ how much top athletes get paid.

A funny   **B** true   **C** famous   **D** real   **E** amazing

19.

Mary liked to dance but felt _____ if someone was watching her.

A happy   **B** bored   **C** awkward   **D** numb
E alone

20.

Thomas can sleep on the sofa, but I'm afraid it's not as _____ a bed.

A paid   **B** new   **C** dirty   **D** old   **E** comfortable

PRACTICE TEST NON VERBAL BATTERY

This section is designed to assess a student's ability to reason and think beyond what they've already been taught. This section includes geometric shapes and figures that aren't normally seen in the classroom.

Figure Matrices

Students are provided with a 2X2 matrix with the image missing in one cell. They have to identify the relationship between the two spatial shapes in the upper line and find a fourth image that has the same correlation with the left shape in the lower line.

Example

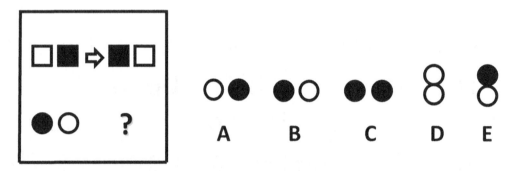

In the upper left box, the image shows a white square and a black square. In the upper right box, the image shows the same squares, but now the white square follows the black square.
The lower left box shows a black circle and a white circle. Which answer choice would go with this image in the same way as the upper images go together?

The image of the answer choice must show two circles but in opposite positions compared to the figures on the left. In other words, the black circle must follow the white circle.
The right answer is "A".

Tips for Figure Matrices

- Consider all the answer choices before selecting one.
- Try to use logic and sequential reasoning.
- Eliminate the logically wrong answers to restrict the options.
- Train yourself to decipher the relationship between different figures and shapes.

1.

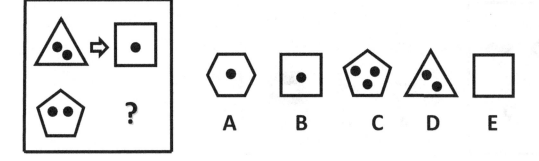

2.

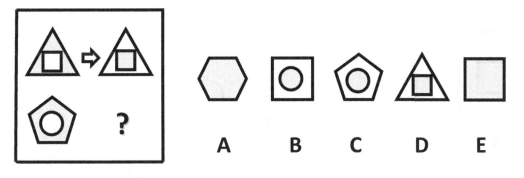

3.

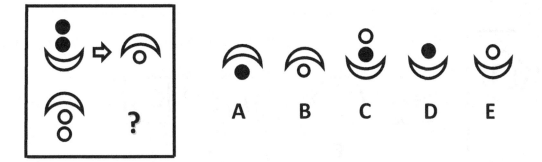

4.

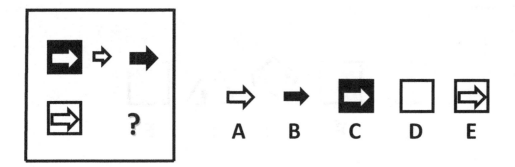

5.

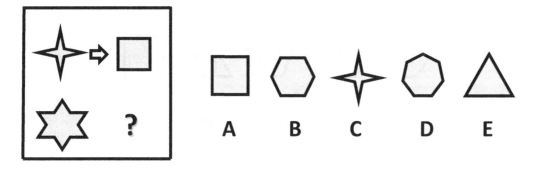

6.

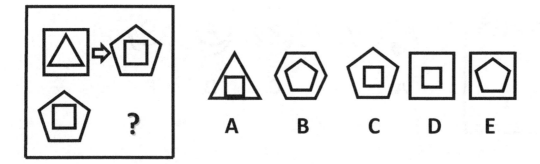

7.

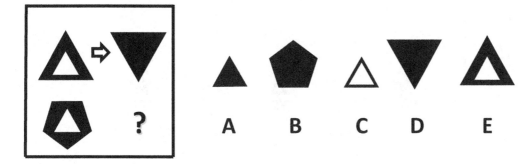

8.

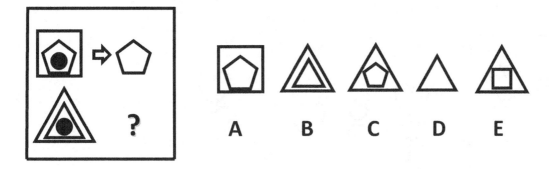

9.

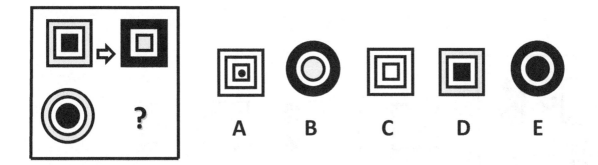

10.

11.

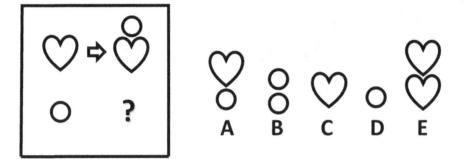

12.

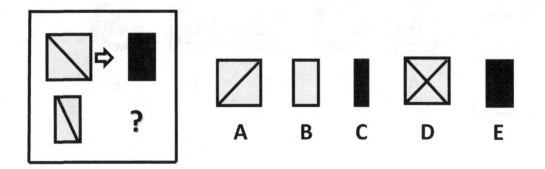

13.

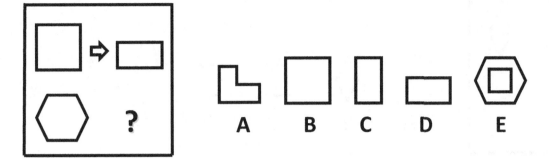

14.

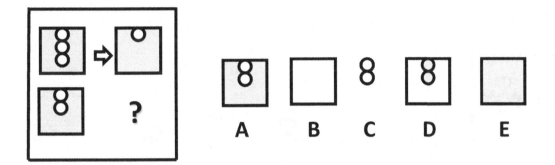

15.

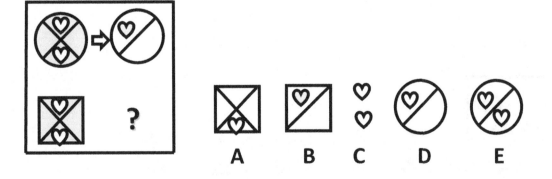

16.

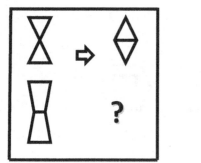

A   B   C   D   E

17.

A   B   C   D   E

18.

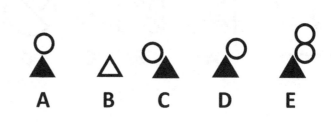

A   B   C   D   E

19.

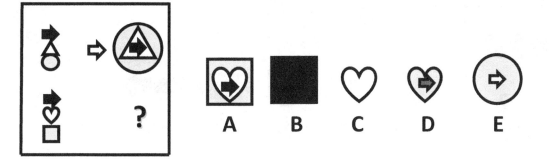

20.

21.

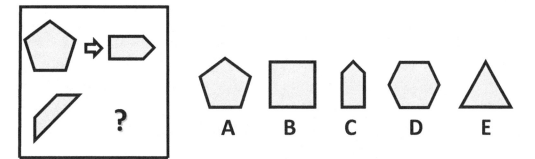

22.

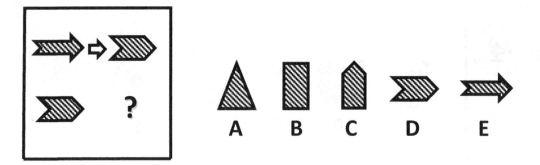

Figure Classification

Students are provided with three shapes and they have to select the answer choice that should be the fourth figure in the set, based on the similarity with the other three figures. The intention is to test the student's ability to recognize similar patterns and to make a rational choice.

Example

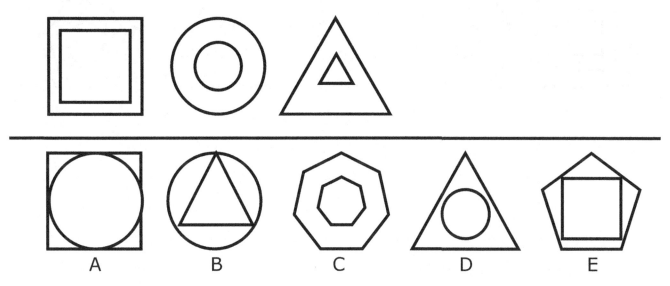

| A | B | C | D | E |

Look at the three pictures on the top. What do these three figures have in common?
You can see a square in a bigger square, a circle in a bigger circle, a triangle in a bigger triangle.
Now, look at the shapes in the row of the answer choices. Which image matches best the three shapes in the top row?

The image of the answer choice must show two identical figures, the smaller one inside the larger one. The right answer is "C" (a smaller heptagon in a larger heptagon).

Tips for Figure Classification

- Be sure to review all answer choices before selecting one.
- Try to use logic and sequential reasoning.
- Try to exclude the obviously wrong options to reduce the answer choices.

1.

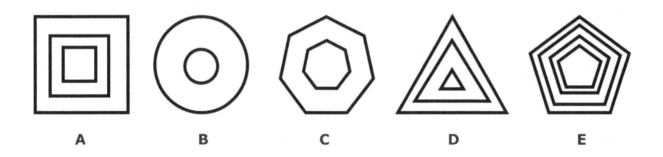

A	B	C	D	E

2.

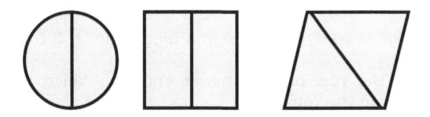

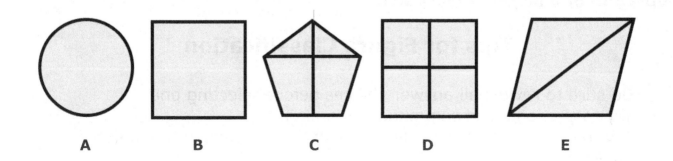

A	B	C	D	E

3.

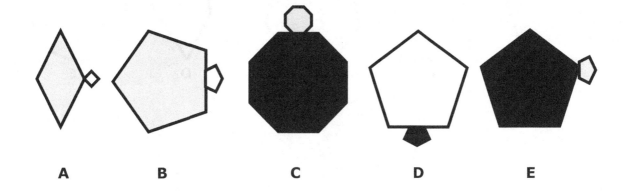

4.

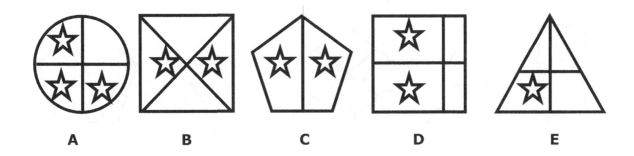

5.

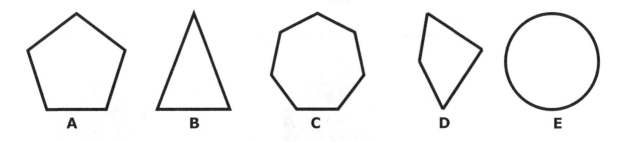

<table>
<tr><td>A</td><td>B</td><td>C</td><td>D</td><td>E</td></tr>
</table>

6.

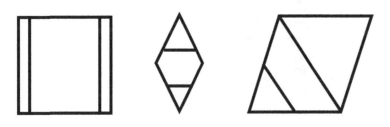

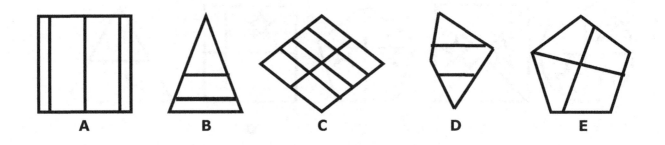

<table>
<tr><td>A</td><td>B</td><td>C</td><td>D</td><td>E</td></tr>
</table>

7.

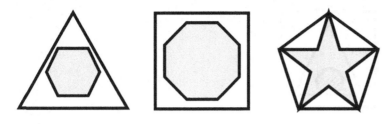

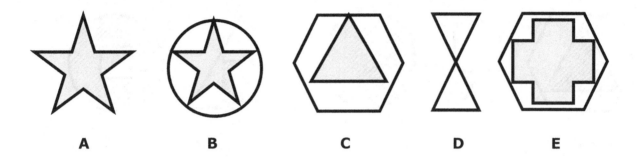

A	B	C	D	E

8.

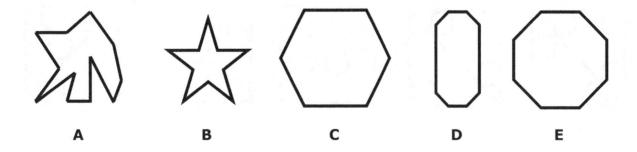

A	B	C	D	E

9.

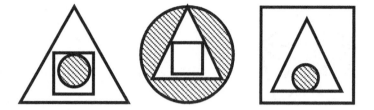

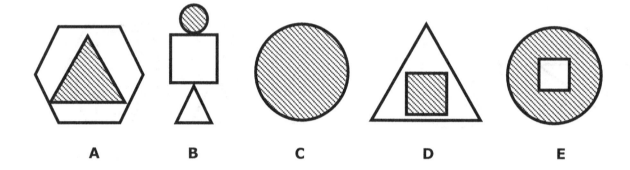

| A | B | C | D | E |

10.

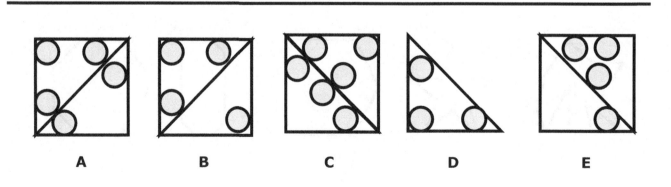

| A | B | C | D | E |

11.

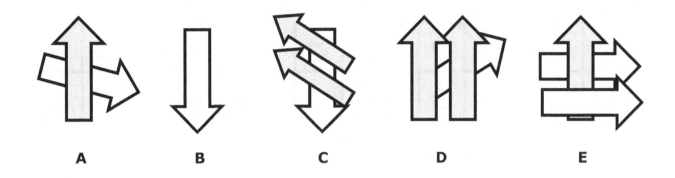

| A | B | C | D | E |

12.

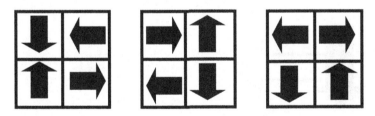

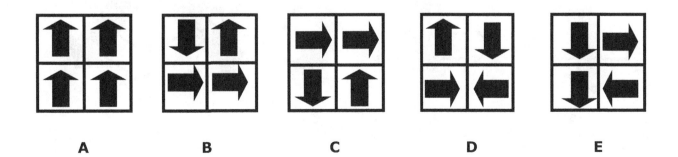

| A | B | C | D | E |

13.

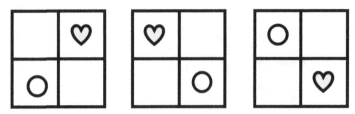

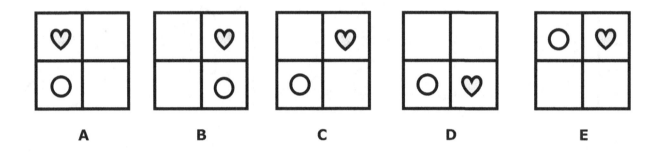

14.

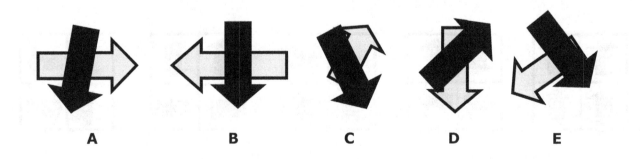

15.

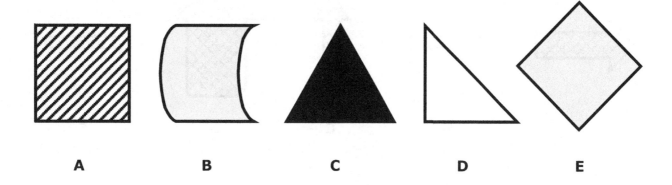

16.

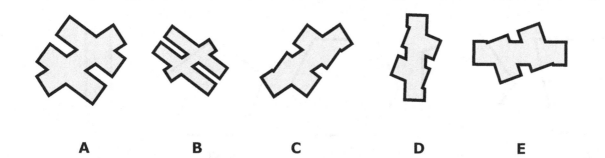

17.

   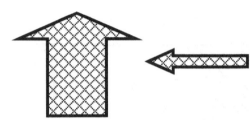

   A   B   C   D   E

18.

   A   B   C   D   E

19.

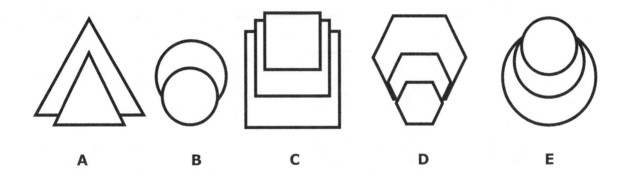

| A | B | C | D | E |

20.

| A | B | C | D | E |

21.

A   B   C   D   E

22.

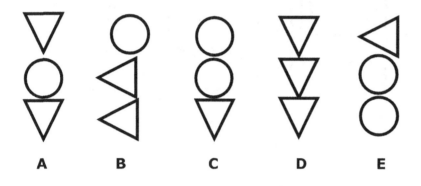

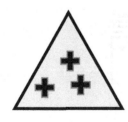 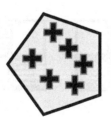  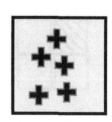 

A   B   C   D   E

Paper Folding

Students need to determine the appearance of a perforated and folded sheet of paper, once opened.

Example

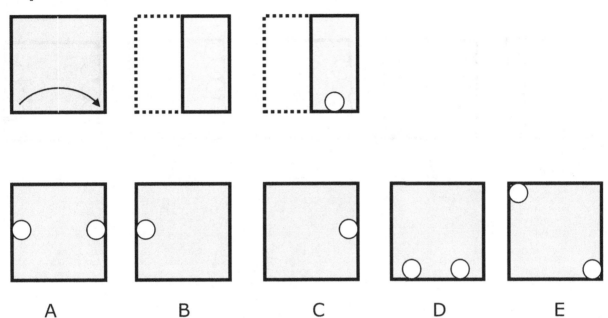

The figures at the top represent a square piece of paper being folded, and the last of these figures has one hole on it.

One of the lower five figures shows where the perforation will be when the paper is fully unfolded. You have to understand which of these images is the right one.

First, the paper was folded horizontally, from left to right.

Then, one hole was punched out. Therefore, when the paper is unfolded the hole will mirror on the left and right side of the sheet.

The right answer is "D".

Tips for Paper Folding

The best way to get ready for these challenging questions is to practice. The patterns that show up on the test can confuse students, so the demonstration of folding and unfolding real paper can be very helpful.

1.

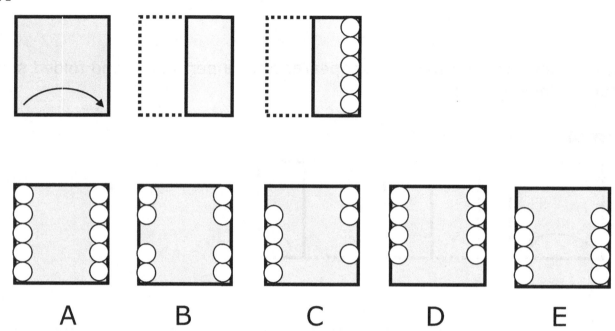

2.

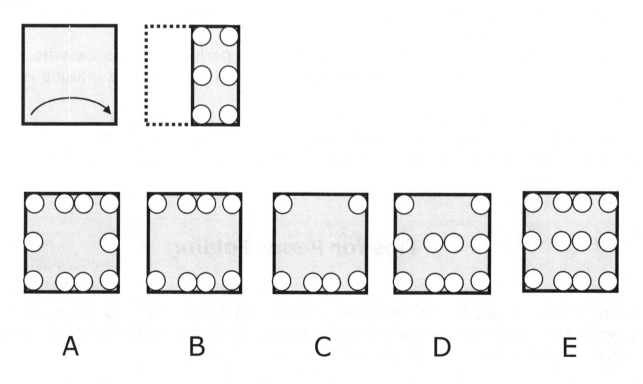

3.

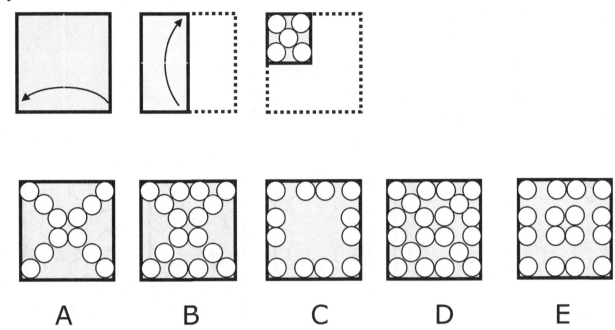

4.

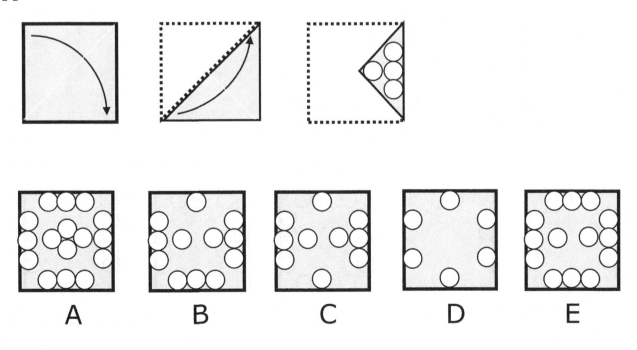

5.

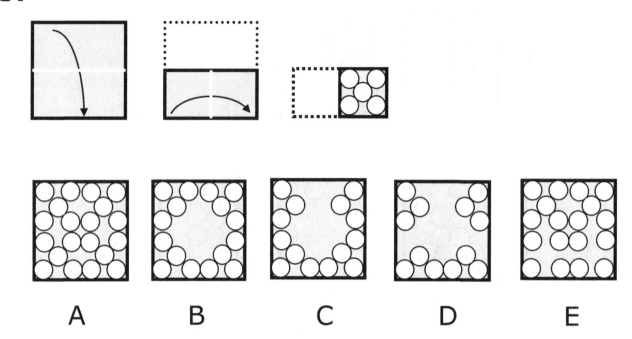

A   B   C   D   E

6.

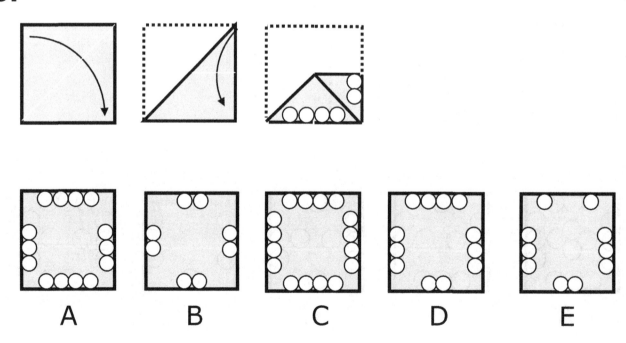

A   B   C   D   E

7.

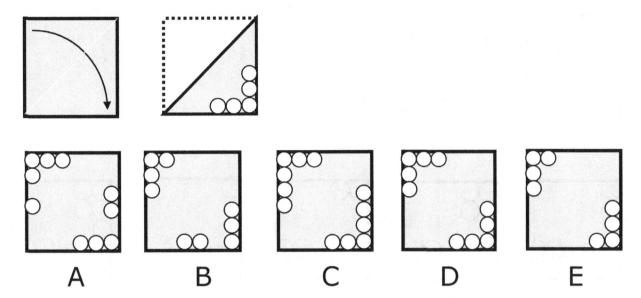

8.

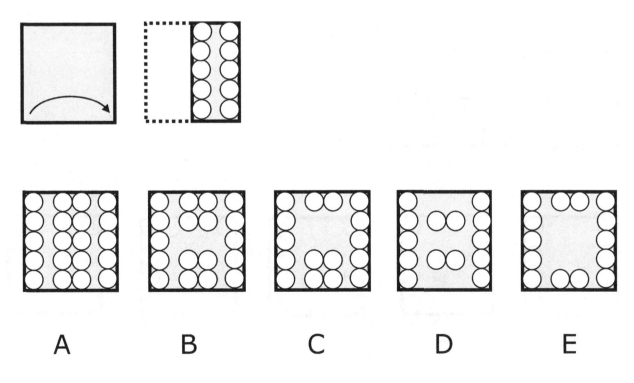

9.

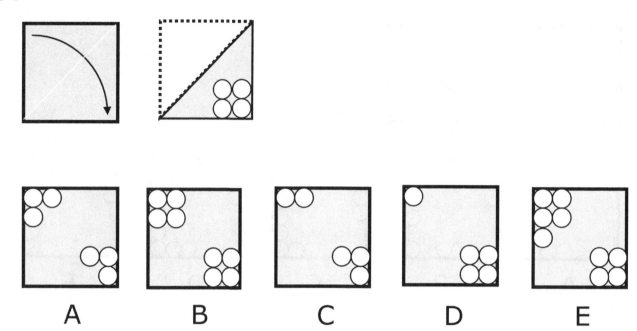

A   B   C   D   E

10.

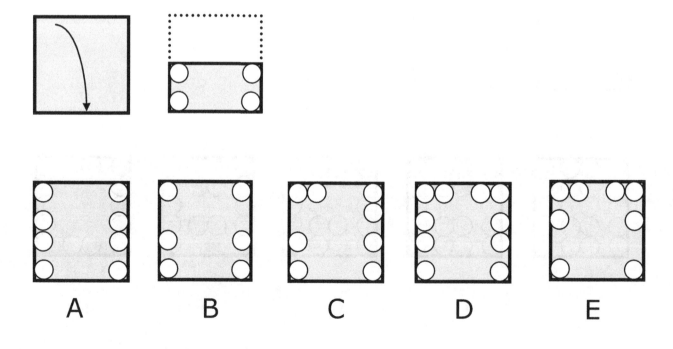

A   B   C   D   E

11.

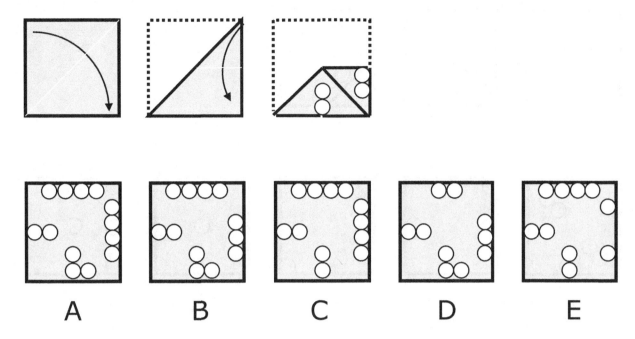

A   B   C   D   E

12.

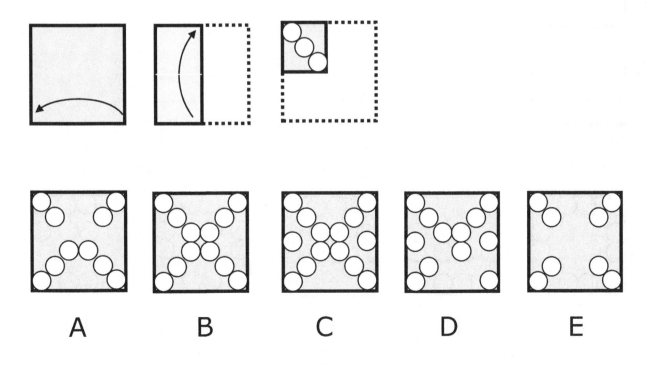

A   B   C   D   E

13.

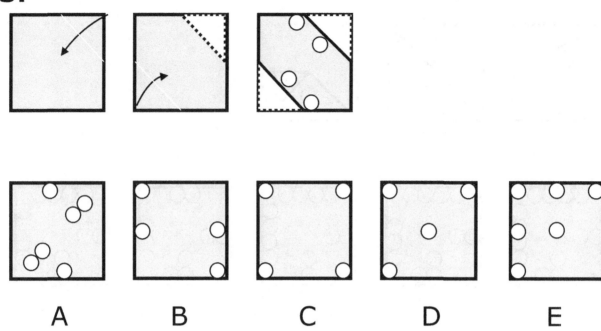

14.

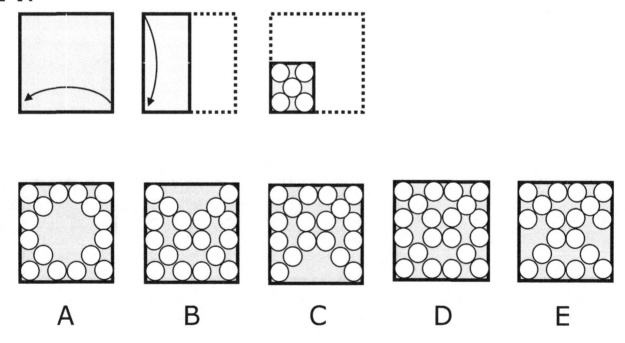

15.

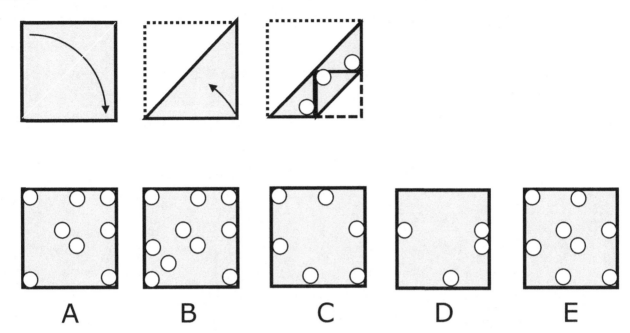

16.

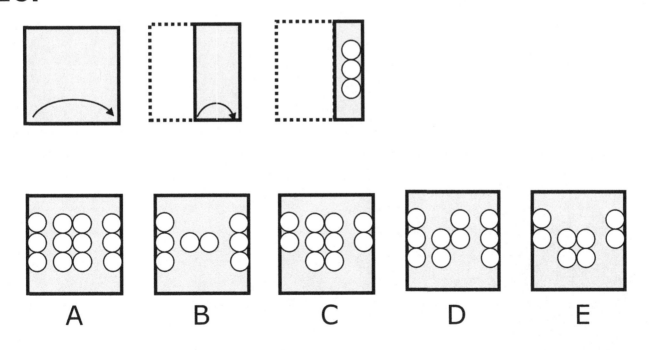

PRACTICE TEST QUANTITATIVE BATTERY

This section introduces abstract reasoning and problem-solving skills to learners and is one of the most challenging sections in the test.

Number Puzzle

Students are required to solve basic mathematical equations. An equation says that two things are equal. It will have an equals sign "=" like this:

$$4 + 2 = 10 - 4$$

The equation says that what is on the left (4 + 2) is equal to what is on the right (10 − 4).

Example 1

$$? - 15 = 4$$

A 10   B 19   C 1   D 7   E 16

- The right side of the equal sign is 4. Which answer should be given in place of the question mark, so that the left side of the equal is also 4?
19 - 15 = 4; 4=4
The right answer is "B".

Example 2

$$? + \blacklozenge = 10$$

$$\blacklozenge = 5$$

A 1   **B** 13   **C** 5   **D** 8   **E** 9

? + 5= 10; 5+5=10; 10=10; the right answer is "C".

Tips for Number Puzzle

- Deeply understand the meaning of "equal", as the purpose is to provide the missing information that will make the two parts of the equation the same.
- Train yourself to solve simple basic equations.
- Practice with numbers and problem solving.

1.

$$? - 12 = 9$$

A 21   **B** 11   **C** 14   **D** 7   **E** 16

2.

$$? + \blacklozenge = 14$$

$$\blacklozenge = 9$$

A 1   **B** 13   **C** 5   **D** 8   **E** 9

3.

$$? + 2 = \blacklozenge$$

$$\blacklozenge = 26$$

A 0   **B** 24   **C** 11   **D** 2   **E** 10

4.

$$? \times 2 = \blacklozenge + 1$$

$$\blacklozenge = 13$$

A 10   **B** 9   **C** 7   **D** 4   **E** 6

5.

$$? - 3 = \blacklozenge + 1$$

$$\blacklozenge = 19$$

A 20   **B** 1   **C** 3   **D** 12   **E** 23

6.

$$12 + 12 = 56 - ?$$

A 2   **B** 32   **C** 30   **D** 6   **E** 1

7.

$$43 = 98 - 4 - ?$$

A 51   **B** 20   **C** 44   **D** 82   **E** 1

8.

$$35 = 60 - 27 + ?$$

A 12   **B** 40   **C** 10   **D** 6   **E** 2

9. $$101 = 1 + 21 + ?$$

A 3   **B** 28   **C** 24   **D** 79   **E** 14

10.

$$77 - 24 = 89 - ?$$

A 22   **B** 2   **C** 21   **D** 36   **E** 19

11.

$$11 + 18 = 41 - ?$$

A 12   **B** 6   **C** 2   **D** 11   **E** 9

12.

$$76 - 12 = 65 - ?$$

A 9   **B** 1   **C** 2   **D** 31   **E** 12

13.

$$? = \blacklozenge + 31$$

$$\blacklozenge = 110$$

A 121   **B** 300   **C** 68   **D** 55   **E** 141

14.

$$? = \blacklozenge \times 3$$

$$\blacklozenge = 21$$

A 30   **B** 10   **C** 63   **D** 25   **E** 31

15.

? = ◆ X 2

◆ = 18

A 62   **B** 36   **C** 37   **D** 50   **E** 4

16.

? = ◆ + 7

25 = ◆ - ●

● = 9

A 52   **B** 18   **C** 41   **D** 44   **E** 1

Number Analogies

In this session, you will see two pairs of numbers and then a number without its pair. The first two pairs of numbers are correlated in some way. Try to find out the correlation between the numbers within each of the pairs. Choose an answer that gives you the third pair of numbers, related to each other in the same way.

Example

[9 → 18]   [5 → 14]   [15 → ?]

A 20   **B** 18   **C** 24   **D** 7   **E** 16

- In the first two sets, you have 9 and 18; 5 and 14. Both numbers (9 and 5), increase by 9 (9+9=18; 5+9=14).
- Apply the same rule to the number 15.

15 + 9 = 24. The right answer is "C".

Tips for Number Analogies

- Step 1: acquire all the information from the two given pairs (relationships, sums, subtractions, etc.).
- Step 2: apply the same rules, relations, formulas that you correctly identified in step 1.
- Step 3: double-check that the rule has been properly applied.

1.

[8 → 30]   [5 → 27]   [15 → ?]

A 22   **B** 37   **C** 18   **D** 19   **E** 16

2.

[12 → 24]   [9 → 18]   [45 → ?]

A 90   **B** 10   **C** 18   **D** 98   **E** 11

3.

[56 → 52]   [9 → 5]   [97 → ?]

A 35   **B** 93   **C** 11   **D** 50   **E** 90

4.

[100 → 25]   [8 → 2]   [48 → ?]

A 11   **B** 10   **C** 50   **D** 12   **E** 20

5.

[4 → 6]   [11 → 20]   [30 → ?]

A 100   **B** 60   **C** 11   **D** 90   **E** 58

6.

[5 → 45]   [8 → 72]   [3 → ?]

A 27   **B** 11   **C** 14   **D** 30   **E** 17

7.

[9 → 73]   [1 → 9]   [4 → ?]

A 10   **B** 17   **C** 33   **D** 19   **E** 21

8.

[20 → 15]   [35 → 30]   [11 → ?]

A 10   **B** 12   **C** 5   **D** 6   **E** 22

9.
[96 → 24]   [36 → 9]   [12 → ?]

A 3   **B** 12   **C** 30   **D** 22   **E** 29

10.
[11 → 15]   [39 → 43]   [76 → ?]

A 19   **B** 10   **C** 36   **D** 91   **E** 80

11.
[20 → 51]   [35 → 66]   [11 → ?]

A 1   **B** 10   **C** 42   **D** 22   **E** 29

12.
[7 → 35]   [25 → 125]   [11 → ?]

A 55   **B** 14   **C** 35   **D** 20   **E** 25

13.
[18 → 2]   [36 → 4]   [99 → ?]

A 16   **B** 10   **C** 30   **D** 11   **E** 12

14.
[98 → 85]   [32 → 19]   [14 → ?]

A 2   **B** 4   **C** 1   **D** 20   **E** 21

15.
[67 → 61]   [21 → 15]   [50 → ?]

A 51   **B** 44   **C** 33   **D** 24   **E** 34

16.
[42 → 6]   [14 → 2]   [28 → ?]

A 1   **B** 12   **C** 30   **D** 4   **E** 20

17.

[69 → 23]   [39 → 13]   [123 → ?]

A 41   **B** 40   **C** 30   **D** 13   **E** 29

18.

[20 → 78]   [4 → 14]   [12 → ?]

A 12   **B** 46   **C** 36   **D** 20   **E** 14

Number Series

Students are provided with a sequence of numbers that follow a pattern. They are required to identify which number should come next in the sequence.

Example 1

$$2 \quad 6 \quad 10 \quad 14 \quad ?$$

A 18   **B** 11   **C** 10   **D** 7   **E** 16

- It's easy to realize that each number in the sequence increases by 4. 2+4=6; 6+4=10; 10+4=14; etc.
- Apply the same rule to the number 14.

14 + 4 = 18. The right answer is "A".

Example 2

$$2 \quad 8 \quad 5 \quad 11 \quad 8 \quad ?$$

A 1   **B** 10   **C** 12   **D** 6   **E** 14

- The sequence follows the rule: +6, -3, +6, -3, +6, etc. 2+6=8; 8-3=5; 5+6=11; 11-3=8; etc.
- Apply the same rule to the number 8.

8 + 6 = 14. The right answer is "E".

Tips for Number Series

- To correctly answer these questions, the student will need to be able to identify the patterns in a sequence of numbers and provide the missing item. Therefore, it is important to practice, working with sequences of numbers.

1.

91   95   99   103   ?

A 107   **B** 110   **C** 100   **D** 99   **E** 111

2.

99   98   97   96   95   ?

A 99   **B** 100   **C** 94   **D** 76   **E** 10

3.

4   14   13   23   22   ?

A 11   **B** 10   **C** 35   **D** 36   **E** 32

4.

11   16   14   19   17   22   20   ?

A 30   **B** 25   **C** 26   **D** 10   **E** 17

5.

    76   **77**   **79**   **82**   **?**

A 99   **B** 79   **C** 89   **D** 100   **E** 86

6.

    10   **0**   **30**   **20**   **50**   **40**   **?**

A 20   **B** 40   **C** 70   **D** 60   **E** 90

7.

    30   **0**   **30**   **0**   **30**   **?**

A 10   **B** 20   **C** 30   **D** 50   **E** 0

8.

    90   **87**   **88**   **85**   **86**   **83**   **?**

A 100   **B** 90   **C** 84   **D** 85   **E** 1

9.

66   61   56   51   46   ?

A 41   **B** 53   **C** 54   **D** 45   **E** 62

10.

22   23   25   26   28   29   ?

A 38   **B** 22   **C** 24   **D** 90   **E** 31

11.

70   72   77   79   84   86   ?

A 92   **B** 91   **C** 81   **D** 83   **E** 95

12.

33   36   32   35   31   34   ?

A 31   **B** 30   **C** 32   **D** 33   **E** 39

13.

4   7   3   6   2   5   ?

A 9   **B** 10   **C** 2   **D** 3   **E** 1

14.

0.3   1.3   2.3   3.3   4.3   5.3   ?

A 0.4   **B** 6.3   **C** 0.35   **D** 4.3   **E** 7.3

15.

0.05   0.10   0.15   0.20   0.25   ?

A 0.3   **B** 0.15   **C** 0.35   **D** 0.30   **E** 0.3

16.

77   69   61   53   45   37   ?

A 29   **B** 24   **C** 36   **D** 52   **E** 31

17.

    2.5   **5**   **7.5**   **10**   **12.5**   **15**   **?**

A 9.5   **B** 12,5   **C** 11   **D** 17.5   **E** 18

18.

    4   **8.5**   **13**   **17.5**   **22**   **26.5**   **?**

A 31   **B** 10.5   **C** 30.5   **D** 37.5   **E** 39.5

ANSWER KEY

Verbal Analogies Practice Test
p.13

1.
Answer: option E
Explanation: actor performs on the stage; skater performs on the rink.

2.
Answer: option C
Explanation: cat eats mouse; bird eats worm.

3.
Answer: option A
Explanation: migraine is a brain disorder; cataract is an eye disorder.

4.
Answer: option B
Explanation: botany studies plants; zoology studies animals.

5.
Answer: option D
Explanation: a switch is used to start the light; a key is used to start the ignition.

6.
Answer: option D
Explanation: the head is connected to the neck; the hand is connected to the wrist.

7.
Answer: option B
Explanation: a sweater is made of yarn; a snowball is made of snow.

8.

Answer: option E

Explanation: surgeon uses scalpel for his working; tailor uses needle for his working.

9.

Answer: option B

Explanation: hand is used to grasp things; reach, is a verb that means, "stretch out an arm to touch or grasp something".

10.

Answer: option C

Explanation: chemist means "one who practices chemistry"; zoologist means "one who practices zoology".

11.

Answer: option A

Explanation: a tree is covered completely by its bark; a bird is covered completely by its feathers.

12.

Answer: option B

Explanation: someone who is naive lacks experience; someone who is illiterate lacks an education.

13.

Answer: option B

Explanation: The noun "darkness" expresses the quality of being dark, and the noun "heaviness" expresses the quality of heavy.

14.

Answer: option D

Explanation: a barber cuts hair; a lumberjack cuts trees.

15.

Answer: option B

Explanation: the life of a God is "eternal"; the life of a "mortal" is "fleeting," or lasting a short time.

16.

Answer: option B

Explanation: "robust" means "healthy, strong". This is a quality usually associated with "young" people; "weak" means "lacking the power to perform physically demanding tasks". This is a quality usually associated with "old" people.

17.

Answer: option E

Explanation: an oasis is surrounded by desert on all sides; an island is a piece of land surrounded by water on all sides.

18.

Answer: option A

Explanation: a "hand" is what a "human" uses to feel and touch things; insects use "feeler" to feel and touch things.

19.

Answer: option B

Explanation: a quality of a comedy is to be humorous; a tragedy is "gloomy", sad.

20.

Answer: option D

Explanation: when you are "thirsty" you drink water; when you are "starving" you eat food.

21.

Answer: option C

Explanation: a "teacher" works inside a "classroom," similar to how a "scientist" works inside a "laboratory."

22.
Answer: option B
Explanation: "drove" is the past tense expression of the verb "drive"; "ate" is the past tense expression of "eat".

23.
Answer: option B
Explanation: a library keeps books for public reading; a museum keeps paintings for public viewing.

24.
Answer: option B
Explanation: someone who is lacking "hair" is "bald"; someone who is lacking "energy" is "anemic."

Verbal Classification Practice Test
p.20

1.
Answer: option B
Explanation: "math", "history", "literature" and "science" are all school subjects.

2.
Answer: option B
Explanation: influenza, measles, chicken pox and ebola are viral diseases.

3.
Answer: option C
Explanation: jump, stop, explore, and run are all verbs.

4.
Answer: option B
Explanation: who, whose, which, what are interrogative pronouns.

5.
Answer: option B
Explanation: sepal, petal, peduncle are all parts of a flower; pistil is also a part of a flower.

6.
Answer: option A
Explanation: good, bad, nice and strange are all adjectives.

7.
Answer: option B
Explanation: north, east, south and west are cardinal points.

8.

Answer: option D

Explanation: brain, liver, heart and stomach are all body organs.

9.

Answer: option B

Explanation: canoe, raft, barge and ship are all types of floating objects built by people that can also be piloted by people.

10.

Answer: option E

Explanation: residence, edifice, lodging and house can be interpreted as pertaining to some sort of building.

11.

Answer: option A

Explanation: coffee, water, wine and tea are liquids.

12.

Answer: option B

Explanation: dove, finch, blackbird are classified as birds in zoological terms; penguin is also classified as bird in zoological terms.

13.

Answer: option C

Explanation: cat, gorilla and tiger are mammals; dolphin is also a mammal.

14.

Answer: option A

Explanation: Arctic, Pacific, Indian are Oceans; Atlantic is also an Ocean.

15.

Answer: option C

Explanation: snake, chameleon, turtle are part of a group of animals known as reptiles; lizard is also a reptile.

16.

Answer: option A

Explanation: car, motorcycle, tractor have wheels; bike has wheels.

17.

Answer: option E

Explanation: English, Spanish, Russian are languages; Italian is also a language.

18.

Answer: option B

Explanation: heptagon, square, triangle are plane figures; hexagon is also a plan figure.

19.

Answer: option C

Explanation: rake, knife, hoe and wheelbarrow are garden tools.

20.

Answer: option A

Explanation: wall, floor, ceiling and door are parts of a room.

Sentence Completion Practice Test
p.26

1.
Answer: option C
Explanation: approve=to officially accept a plan, proposal etc.

2.
Answer: option A
Explanation: exploit= to use something as fully and effectively as possible.

3.
Answer: option D
Explanation: draw on something=to use information, knowledge, or experience that you have learned in the past.

4.
Answer: option C
Explanation: utilize= to use something that is available to you, for a practical purpose.

5.
Answer: option B
Explanation: consume=to use time, energy, goods etc.

6.
Answer: option C
Explanation: inject=to put liquid, especially a drug, into someone's body by using a special needle

7.
Answer: option D
Explanation: proud=feeling pleased about something that you have done.

8.
Answer: option C
Explanation: afford = to provide something or allow something to happen.

9.
Answer: option B
Explanation: never = not at any time, or not once.

10.
Answer: option E
Explanation: anticipate=to do something before someone else.

11.
Answer: option C
Explanation: expel = to officially force someone to leave a school or organization.

12.
Answer: option A
Explanation: surprise=an unexpected or astonishing event, fact, etc.

13.
Answer: option D
Explanation: join = connect.

14.
Answer: option D
Explanation: active=always busy doing things, especially physical or mental activities.

15.
Answer: option E
Explanation: dormant=it has not erupted for a long time.

16.

Answer: option C

Explanation: reveal = to make known something that was previously secret or unknown.

17.

Answer: option D

Explanation: care: the process of protecting someone or something and providing what that person or thing needs.

18.

Answer: option E

Explanation: amazing = surprising.

19.

Answer: option C

Explanation: awkward = making you feel embarrassed so that you are not sure what to do or say.

20.

Answer: option E

Explanation: comfortable = making you feel physically relaxed.

Figure Matrices Practice Test
p.35

1.
Answer: option A

Explanation: the right shapes have one more side and one less black circle inside.

2.
Answer: option C

Explanation: the smaller shape becomes grey; the larger shape becomes white.

3.
Answer: option D

Explanation: the half-moon shape point in opposite direction; the two circles become one, the remaining circle changes color and position in relation to the half-moon.

4.
Answer: option A

Explanation: the larger shape is removed.

5.
Answer: option B

Explanation: four-pointed star: square (four-sided) = six-pointed star: hexagon (six-sided).

6.
Answer: option B

Explanation: (triangle in square: square in pentagon) = (square in pentagon: pentagon in hexagon). Larger shapes have 1 more side than the smaller inside shapes. The shapes on the right have one more side than the figures on the left.

7.
Answer: option B
Explanation: the smaller inside shape is removed; the larger shape is rotated.

8.
Answer: option D
Explanation: larger shape and black circle are removed.

9.
Answer: option B
Explanation: the larger shape becomes black; the smaller shape becomes grey.

10.
Answer: option B
Explanation: the grey triangle is removed.

11.
Answer: option B
Explanation: addition of a circle on top of the left figure.

12.
Answer: option C
Explanation: half width without diagonal and the color becomes black.

13.
Answer: option A
Explanation: four-sided shapes and six-sided shapes.

14.
Answer: option E
Explanation: two white circles are removed.

15.
Answer: option B
Explanation: (four grey parts of a circle with two white hearts: two white parts of a circle with one grey heart) = (four grey parts of a square with two white hearts: two white parts of a square with one grey heart).

16.
Answer: option E
Explanation: 180-degree rotation.

17.
Answer: option C
Explanation: addition of a grey heart over the figure on the left.

18.
Answer: option E
Explanation: one black triangle is removed.

19.
Answer: option A
Explanation: combos of same shapes, one on top of the other (to the left), one inside the other (to the right)

20.
Answer: option C
Explanation: the shape within moves to the left.

21.
Answer: option B
Explanation: (five-sided shape: five-sided shape) = (for-sided shape: four-sided shape).

22.
Answer: option B
Explanation: (eight-sided shape: six-sided shape) = (six-sided shape: four-sided shape) (two sides less)

Figure Classification Practice Test
p.44

1.
Answer: option E.
Explanation: four equal shapes, one inside the other.

2.
Answer: option E
Explanation: each figure is divided into two equal parts.

3.
Answer: option C
Explanation: rhombus above larger rhombus, pentagon above larger pentagon, circle above larger circle, octagon above larger octagon.

4.
Answer: option D
Explanation: one vertical line and one horizontal line inside each shape; two stars inside each shape.

5.
Answer: option D
Explanation: four-sided shapes.

6.
Answer: option D
Explanation: four-sided shapes divided into three parts.

7.
Answer: option E

Explanation: square is a four-sided polygon; octagon is an eight-sided polygon (double). Pentagon is a five-sided polygon; star is a ten-sided shape (double). Triangle is a three-sided polygon; hexagon is a six-sided polygon (double). Hexagon is a six-sided polygon; cross shape is a twelve-sided shape (double).

8.
Answer: option A

Explanation: twelve-sided shapes.

9.
Answer: option B

Explanation: combos of triangle, circle, square.

10.
Answer: option B

Explanation: three grey circles lie on the left side of a diagonal; one grey circle lies on the right side of a diagonal.

11.
Answer: option A

Explanation: two arrows, one grey and one white.

12.
Answer: option D

Explanation: four black arrows in each square, each one with a different orientation.

13.
Answer: option C

Explanation: grey heart and white circle are across from another.

14.
Answer: option B

Explanation: arrows cross at right angles.

15.
Answer: option B
Explanation: rounded shapes.

16.
Answer: option A
Explanation: same rotated figures, same sizes.

17.
Answer: option A
Explanation: figures of same size and color.

18.
Answer: option A
Explanation: four-sided shapes.

19.
Answer: option D
Explanation: three figures; the size of designs is increasing gradually from the bottom to the top.

20.
Answer: option A
Explanation: in every figure, there are four squares and only one square has straight horizontal lines.

21.
Answer: option B
Explanation: one circle and two triangles; one triangle must be in the middle.

22.
Answer: option A
Explanation: in all figures there are as many cross signs as there are sides in the figure.

Paper Folding Practice Test
p.56

1.
Answer: option A

2.
Answer: option E

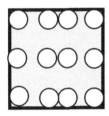

3.
Answer: option D

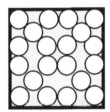

4.
Answer: option A

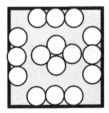

5.
Answer: option A

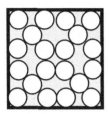

6.
Answer: option C

7
Answer: option D

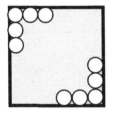

8.
Answer: option A

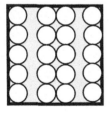

9.
Answer: option B

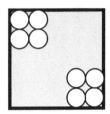

10.
Answer: option A

11.
Answer: option C

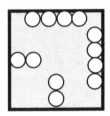

12.
Answer: option B

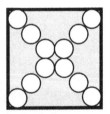

13.
Answer: option A

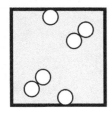

14.
Answer: option D

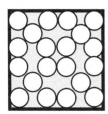

15.
Answer: option E

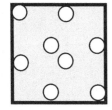

16.
Answer: option A

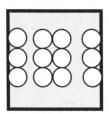

Number Puzzle Practice Test
p.67

1.
Answer: option A
Explanation: 21-12=9; 9=9

2.
Answer: option C
Explanation: 5+9=14; 14=14

3.
Answer: option B
Explanation: 24+2=26; 26=26

4.
Answer: option C
Explanation: 7X2=13+1; 14=14

5.
Answer: option E
Explanation: 23-3=19+1; 20=20

6.
Answer: option B
Explanation: 12+12=56-32; 24=24

7.
Answer: option A
Explanation: 43=98-4-51; 43=43

8.
Answer: option E
Explanation: 35=60-27+2; 35=33+2; 35=35

9.
Answer: option D
Explanation: 101=1+21+79; 101=22+79; 101=101

10.
Answer: option D
Explanation: 77-24=89-36; 53=53

11.
Answer: option A
Explanation: 11+18=41-12; 29=29

12.
Answer: option B
Explanation: 76-12 =65-1; 64=64

13.
Answer: option E
Explanation: 141=110+31; 141=141

14.
Answer: option C
Explanation: 63=21X3; 63=63

15.
Answer: option B
Explanation: 36=18X2; 36=36

16.
Answer: option C
Explanation: ◆ = 25+9; ◆ =34; 41=34+7

Number Analogies Practice Test
p.73

1.
Answer: option B
Explanation: 8+22=30   5+22=27   15+22=37

2.
Answer: option A
Explanation: 12X2=24   9X2=18   45X2=90

3.
Answer: option B
Explanation: 56-4=52   9-4=5   97-4=93

4.
Answer: option D
Explanation: 100:4=25   8:4=2   48:4=12

5.
Answer: option E
Explanation: 4X2=8; 8-2=6   11X2=22; 22-2=20   30X2=60; 60-2=58

6.
Answer: option A
Explanation: 5X9=45   8X9=72   3X9=27

7.
Answer: option C
Explanation: 9X8=72; 72+1=73   1X8=8; 8+1=9   4X8=32; 32+1=33

8.
Answer: option D
Explanation: 20-5=15   35-5=30   11-5=6

9.
Answer: option A
Explanation: 96:4=24   36:4=9   12:4=3

10.
Answer: option E
Explanation: 11+4=15   39+4=43   76+4=80

11.
Answer: option C
Explanation: 20+31=51   35+31=66   11+31=42

12.
Answer: option A
Explanation: 7X5=35   25X5=125   11X5=55

13.
Answer: option D
Explanation: 18:9=2   36:9=4   99:9=11

14.
Answer: option C
Explanation: 98-13=85   32-13=19   14-13=1

15.
Answer: option B
Explanation: 67-6=61   21-6=15   50-6=44

16.
Answer: option D
Explanation: 42:7=6   14:7=2   28:7=4

17.
Answer: option A
Explanation: 69:3=23   39:3=13   123:3=41

18.
Answer: option B
Explanation: 20X4=80; 80-2=78   4X4=16; 16-2=14
            12X4=48; 48-2=46

Number Series Practice Test
p.79

1.
Answer: option A
Explanation: +4, +4, +4, +4, etc. 91+4=95; 95+4=99; 99+4=103; 103+4=107

2.
Answer: option C
Explanation: -1, -1, -1, -1, -1, etc.

3.
Answer: option E
Explanation: +10, -1, +10, -1, +10, etc.

4.
Answer: option B
Explanation: +5, -2, +5, -2, +5, -2, +5, etc.

5.
Answer: option E
Explanation: +1, +2, +3, +4, etc.

6.
Answer: option C
Explanation: -10, +30, -10, +30, -10, +30, etc.

7.
Answer: option E
Explanation: -30, +30, -30, +30, -30, etc.

8.
Answer: option C
Explanation: -3, +1, -3, +1, -3, +1, etc.

9.
Answer: option A
Explanation: -5, -5, -5, -5, -5, etc.

10.
Answer: option E
Explanation: +1, +2, +1, +2, +1, +2, etc.

11.
Answer: option B
Explanation: +2, +5, +2, +5, +2, +5, etc.

12.
Answer: option B
Explanation: +3, -4, +3, -4, +3, -4, etc.

13.
Answer: option E
Explanation: +3, -4, +3, -4, +3, -4, etc.

14.
Answer: option B
Explanation: +1, +1, +1, +1, +1, +1, etc.

15.
Answer: option D
Explanation: +0.05, +0.05, +0.05, +0.05, +0.05, +0.05, etc.

16.
Answer: option A
Explanation: -8, -8, -8, -8, -8, -8, etc.

17.
Answer: option D
Explanation: +2.5, +2.5, +2.5, +2.5, +2.5, +2.5, etc.

18.
Answer: option A
Explanation: +4.5, +4.5, +4.5, +4.5, +4.5, +4.5, etc.

HOW TO DOWNLOAD 54 BONUS QUESTIONS

Thank you for reading this book, we hope you really enjoyed it and found it very helpful.

PLEASE LEAVE US A REVIEW ON THE WEBSITE WHERE YOU PURCHASED THIS BOOK!

By leaving a review, you give us the opportunity to improve our work.

A GIFT FOR YOU!

FREE ONLINE ACCESS TO 54 BONUS PRACTICE QUESTIONS.

Follow this link:

https://www.skilledchildren.com/download-cogat-grade-5-test-prep.php

You will find a PDF to download: please insert this PASSWORD: 010366

Nicole Howard and the SkilledChildren.com Team

www.skilledchildren.com

Made in the USA
Las Vegas, NV
18 April 2024

88834180R00063